I AM

I am

awareness poems.
By Michael Grinder

Though it seems that you are
traveling towards another,
the journey is within yourself.
And though it seems you love
another, it is self-love expressing.
And what is beautiful is that
you venture with the knowledge of
the risk involved — the possible
and painful hurt.
And even if the risk is lost
you will journey again.
Though the risk remains,
now you know that you have the
capacity to love.

MY LIFE IS ONE OF INNER TRAVEL TOWARDS MYSELF with OTHERS

IT TAKES TWO TO BE
AT ONE. WHEN I AM AT ONE
WITH MYSELF I CAN
BE THE OTHER.

the BASIS of
COMMUNICATING
in a relationship
is the ability of
each person to
BE the OTHER.

the KEY is my
AWARENESS of when
I can be the OTHER
and when
I cannot.

and my SUCCESS
in COMMUNICATING
is trying to be
the OTHER
ONLY
WHEN
I CAN.

the meaning of *life* is found in the JOY of celebrating it.

THERE ARE TWO DEGREES OF AWARENES
OF "HOW I FEEL".
I CAN BE AWARE OF HOW I FEEL
TOWARD
another
and

I CAN BE AWARE OF HOW I FEEL
TOWARD MYSELF.

WHEN I EXPERIENCE THE FIRST
I FEEL CAUSED.
when I experience the secon
I feel responsibility
and FREEDOM.

The THRILL of a relationship is
in the RISK of not knowing.

The STRUGGLE of a relationship
is in adapting from what each
pictured the other to be and how
each thought he would be
pictured by the other.

The JOY of a relationship is in
learning to expand one's past
expectations.

And the SECRET
of a relationship
is that the relationship
is really
with one's
OWN SELF.

YOU ME

May I EXPERIENCE the liberation of **my**SELF in allowing the FREEDOM of **OTHERS**

Sometimes HOW
I REACT
to what happens
is more important
than what
ACTUALLY
HAPPENS.

inner peace is lived when
the HOPE of the future doesn't
blind my life
    in the PRESENT

is anxiety
not the result
of having
EXPECTATIONS?

N LISTENING TO YOU, I NEED SOME CLARIFICATIONS; ARE YOU ASKING ME A QUESTION, AND THEREFORE WOULD LIKE A RESPONSE FROM ME, OR ARE YOU EXPRESSING YOURSELF and JUST wanting me to LISTEN?

I have no interest in findin out *why I am",* just *how I am;"*

I WANT TO KNOW AND EXPERIENCE how I am with **you.**

the amount that
I am in the NOW
is the amount that
I am healthy.

When I am
in the NOW
my thinking and feeling and doing
are UNITED...
as when I read a book...

I AM thinking, feeling and
doing a book.

THINKING FEE
KING FEELING

my living is trying to
ENVISION the HOPES of the FUTURE
without being blinded to the
JOYS of the
PRESENT

When I was younger I and Knowledge

ranted to be older

wiser with

NOW that I

am older I realize

that

O KNOW IS TO NEVER EXPERIENCE

AGAIN."

-- Mari

I KNOW the SUNSET is there...
BUT
I am so frustrated when I
try to share it...
BECAUSE
what I am trying to share is
not the sunset itself, but
MY EXPERIENCING MYSELF
    EXPERIENCING the SUNSET.

There is a difference between being "HONEST" and being "OPEN".

HONESTY has to do with my feelings about people and things outside of me.

OPENNESS has to do with my reactions to my own self.

when I experience a FEELING
and express it in a
thought
I cause a gap by
means of the
TRANSLATION.

love
IS HOW I FEEL
ABOUT THE
OTHER.

LIKE is how i feel about me being
WITH THE OTHER.
Usually I LOVE THOSE i like
but I don't like all those I LOVE.

meetings with old friends
are flashes back to
where I used to be

HAVE SUCH

SURGING OF FREEDOM WHEN I REALIZE

I PRODUCE
MY OWN ANXIETY.

at best it is triggered from
the outside, but never caused.

SHOULDS
are
expectations
that I allowed
others to assign
to me by means
of the roles
they said I have

I LISTEN BEST WHEN LEAST THREATENED, and I AM LEAST THREATENED when LISTENING TO SOMEONE TALK IN TERMS OF HIMSELF instead of ME.

when I'm experiencing a
"thinking-patterned" life style
I find myself saying, "I should.

When I am in a "FEELING-PATTERNED" life style I find myself saying, "I WANT."

growth

growth is often an outcome of STRUGGLING with myself by RISKING into new areas.

But the risks are of two KINDS.

the FIRST: when I can concentrate on what I am working on as well as be aware that I AM SCARED. THIS IS AN APPROPRIATE RISK AND LEADS TO GROWTH.

THE SECOND: when I am overwhelmed by the confusion that I am experiencing and I cannot focus on the area. THIS IS OVER-RISK and leads to feelings of "BEING LOST"

when I Feel that
my FREEDOM
(power and mobility)
depends on another
then I AM NOT WITH
MYSELF.
Because the responsibility
of that freedom is too
awesome.

AS A PARENT:
If I let "what satisfies me"
and what makes me feel "comfortable" be the standards of acceptable behavior for Krista, then I am not only attempting to REPRODUCE myself, but closing the possibility of having an INTIMATE RELATIONSHIP with a contrasting personality.

THERE IS NO "WHY" TO MY FEELINGS, ONLY A "**How.**"

a baby is like
a butterfly. When it
is captured it no
longer possesses that
which I hoped to
obtain by holding it.

Krista

the uniqueness of Krista
as an infant is her
bubbling spontaneity.
She is at one with her
surroundings. For Krista
there is no time gap
separating her inside and
the outside of her. Her
smile is not limited to
her face nor is a wet
diaper felt only by her bottom.

a conversation is like a
       painting
in that there is a
foreground (what is spoken)
and a background
(the emotions felt).   •
And only when I see BOTH,
do I see the WHOLE.

my BROTHER is one
who accepts and
appreciates my "NO"
as well as he does
my "yes".

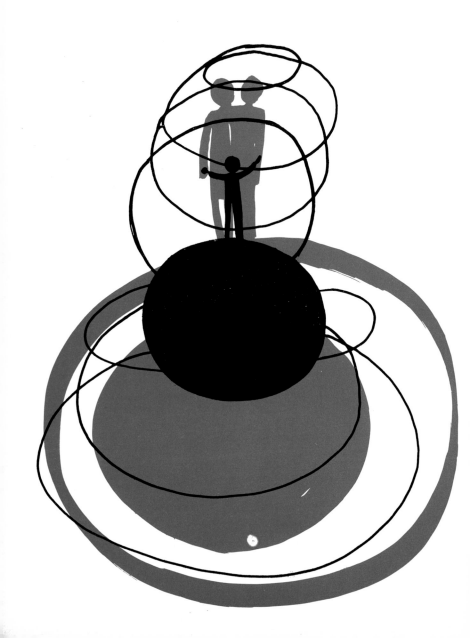

emotional maturity
is not a change in
the circumstances
in my life style,
but the ability to feel
that I am powerful
enough to change if I want to.

I KNOW HOW I WOULD LIKE MYSELF TO BE WITH OTHERS.

I WOULD LIKE TO GIVE THEM "ROOM TO GROW". I AM REALIZING THAT HOW I AM TOWARDS OTHERS IS A MIRROR REFLECTING HOW I AM WITH MYSELF.

WHEN I AM IMPOSING MYSELF UPON OTHERS I AM ACTUALLY REFLECTING MY RESTRICTION AND LACK OF FREEDOM THAT I HAVE INSIDE.

my OPEN

NESS

is the ability to change my expectations.

my ability to
GROW is my ability
BOTH to be involved with my
LIFE and REMOVED enough to
observe. then I can choose
appropriate risks to compare my
LIFE STYLE.

the difference between **awareness** and theraphy is an ability to be interested in **HOW I am** instead of **why** I AM.

the fog between myself and me clears as I see my reflection through the eyes of another.

the more "I AM I"
the less I have to impose
myself on others for them
to be according to
my expectations.

My FEAR of being without expectations is the risk of just BEING without being a certain someone.

I will not be able to judge myself on how well or poorly I am doing if I haven't anticipated.

Am I worthwhile enough just to be ME... to be whatever I am or may be?...

I once saw life as a struggle
to some yet-to-be defined goal.
now I see the search as the end
in itself.
And it is in the fleeting moments
of glimpsing the end
as being yet the beginning that
I realize the NOW.